FAKE
NEWS
MEDIA

The World of Donald Trump
In His Own Words

Compiled and Edited by

Paul Harris

Born in Wolverhampton, England in
1967, Paul Harris is the author of three novels
and one work of non-fiction. Much of his
earlier work was published in the small press
magazines of the 90's, including "Good Stories"
magazine in December 1994 and in
"Staple" magazine the following summer.

ISBN-13: 978-1544096841
ISBN-10: 1544096844

"Nuclear holocaust would be like no other." So speaks the controversial 45th president of the United States of America, and who could doubt the profundity of his words?

Donald Trump is adored by some and vilified by others but his speeches, pronouncements and plentiful Twitter feeds are transmitted around the globe on an almost daily basis. They are listened to and read by all. They are the keys that unlock the doors to a fascinating mind. His words shape our living history and will be remembered long after the words of wiser men and women are long forgotten. Here are just a few examples of those words.

Themes:

1. Political Issues .9
In which Mr Trump expounds on his political ambitions, his presidential campaign, his victory, and the failings of his rivals.

2. International Relations .36
In which Mr Trump gives us his thoughts on Russia, nuclear holocaust, uranium, Brexit, NATO, and North Korea.

3. Immigration .55
In which Mr Trump clarifies his position on Mexico, Sweden, Syria, and the Great Southern Border Wall.

4. Trade .73
In which Mr Trump explains the trade deficit, protectionism, and how he intends to deal with America's trade partners.

5. Gender Issues .82
In which Mr Trump provides an insight into women, romance, sex and homosexuality

6. The Middle-East .87
In which Mr Trump sheds more light on the US relationship with Iraq, Iran, Syria, Israel and the war on terror.

7. Environmental Issues .98
In which Mr Trump expresses his opinions on matters concerning global warming and climate change.

8. The Media .100
In which Mr Trump elucidates on television, the press, celebrity culture, fake news and Rosie O'Donnel

"I guess I can't be doing so badly, because I'm president, and you're not."

Time Magazine
March 2017

Political Issues

In which Mr Trump expounds on his political ambitions, his presidential campaign, his victory, and the failings of his rivals.

On his political ambitions:

"I have no intention of ever running for president."

Time Magazine
14th September 1987

"To be blunt, people would vote for me. They just would. Why? Maybe because I'm so good looking."

The New York Times
19th September 1999

"Well, if I ever ran for office, I'd do better as a Democrat than as a Republican, and that's not because I'd be more liberal, because I'm conservative. But the working guy would elect me. He likes me. When I walk down the street, those cabbies start yelling out their windows."

Playboy Magazine
March 1990

"I think I'm a very honest guy and, in fact, maybe too honest to be a politician."

ABC News
28th November 1999

"I will be the greatest jobs president that God ever created. I tell you that.
I'll bring back our jobs from China, from Mexico, from Japan, from so many places. I'll bring back our jobs, and I'll bring back our money."

Presidential Announcement Speech
New York
16th June 2015

On the presidential campaign:

"I love polls. And somebody said, 'He talks about polls, and the other people don't.' That's because I'm winning. The other people are losing."

Campaign Rally
Las Vegas
8th October 2015

"We should just cancel the election and just give it to Trump."

Campaign Rally
Toledo, Ohio
27th October 2016

"And, you know, there's a real good chance, no matter what happens, I won't win. Because, you know, one of these blood-sucking politicians who's been bullshitting people for years will end up, you know, getting elected."

Republican Party Rally
Las Vegas
28th April 2011

"Nobody thought I was gonna run. They said, 'Why would he run? He's got a great life, he's got a beautiful family, he's got a great company.'"

Campaign Rally
South Carolina
19th October 2015

"And did you notice that baby was crying through half of the speech and I didn't get angry? Not once. Did you notice that? That baby was driving me crazy. I didn't get angry once because I didn't want to insult the parents for not taking the kid out of the room."

Political Rally
Iowa
28th April 2015

"Actually, I was only kidding. You can get that baby out of here. Don't worry, I think she really believed me that I love having a baby crying while I'm speaking."

Campaign Rally
2nd August 2016

"I don't know what hotel this is, but you ought to try turning on the air conditioning or we're not going to get you paid."

Campaign Rally
Hotel Roanoke, Virginia
26th July 2016

"I've had a beautiful, I've had a flawless campaign. You'll be writing books about this campaign."

29th July 2016

"We won with young, we won with old, we won with highly educated, we won with poorly educated. I love the poorly educated."

23rd February 2016
Nevada

On dealing with protestors at his campaign rallies:

"I love the old days, you know? You know
what I hate? There's a guy totally disruptive,
throwing punches, we're not allowed to punch
back anymore. ... I'd like to punch him in the
face, I'll tell ya."

Campaign Rally
Nevada
22nd February 2016

"There may be somebody with tomatoes in
the audience. If you see somebody getting
ready to throw a tomato, knock the crap out of
them, would you? Seriously. Okay? Just
knock the hell… I promise you, I will pay for
the legal fees."

Campaign Rally
Cedar Rapids, Iowa
1st February 2016

"That was so great. Who was the person who
did that [tackled a protestor]? Put up your
hand, put up your hand. Bring that person up
here. I love that."

Campaign Rally
South Carolina
16th February 2016

On winning the presidential election:

"We did it! Thank you to all of my great supporters, we just officially won the election (despite all of the distorted and inaccurate media)."

Twitter
19th December 2016

"Well, we all did it, together! I hope the "MOVEMENT" fans will go to D.C. on Jan 20th for the swearing in. Let's set the all time record!"

Twitter
16th December 2016

"People are pouring into Washington in record numbers. Bikers for Trump are on their way. It will be a great Thursday, Friday and Saturday!"

Twitter
17th January 2016

"There will be plenty of movie and entertainment stars. All the dress shops are sold out in Washington. It's hard to find a great dress for this inauguration."

The New York Times
9th January 2017

"In addition to winning the Electoral College in a landslide, I won the popular vote if you deduct the millions of people who voted illegally"

Twitter
27th November 2016

"Happy New Year to all, including to my many enemies and those who have fought me and lost so badly they just don't know what to do. Love!"

Twitter
31st December 2016

"The Democrats made up and pushed the Russian story as an excuse for running a terrible campaign. Big advantage in Electoral College & lost!"

Twitter
20th March 2017

"Can you imagine if the election results were the opposite and WE tried to play the Russia/CIA card. It would be called conspiracy theory!"

Twitter
12th December 2016

"I did what was an almost an impossible thing to do for a Republican-easily won the Electoral College! Now Tax Returns are brought up again?"

Twitter
16th April 2017

"For those who have chosen not to support me in the past, of which there were a few people, I'm reaching out to you for your guidance and your help so that we can work together and unify our great country."

Election Victory Speech
New York
9th November 2016

On his political rivals:

"I'm the most successful person ever to run for the presidency, by far. Nobody's ever been more successful than me. I'm the most successful person ever to run. Ross Perot isn't successful like me. Romney? I have a Gucci store that's worth more than Romney."

Des Moines Register
2nd June 2015

Jeb Bush:

"Jeb said, 'We were safe with my brother. We were safe.' Well, the World Trade Center just fell down! Now, am I trying to blame him? I'm not blaming anybody. But the World Trade Center came down. So when he said we were safe, that's not safe."

Fox News
18th October 2015

"Jeb Bush has to like Mexican illegals because of his wife."

Twitter
4th April 2015

Carly Fiorina:

"Look at that face! Would anyone vote for that? Can you imagine that, the face of your next president? I mean, she's a woman, and I'm not supposed to say bad things, but really, folks, come on. Are we serious?"

Rolling Stone
9th September 2015

"I think she's got a beautiful face and I think she's a beautiful woman."

CNN
16th September 2015

Rand Paul:

"I never attacked him on his looks, and believe me, there's plenty of subject matter right there."

CNN
16th September 2015

Rick Santorum:

"I have a big plane, he doesn't."

Des Moines Register
8th April 2015

Rick Perry:

"He's doing very poorly in the polls. He put on glasses so people will think he's smart, and it just doesn't work. You know, people can see through the glasses."

Political Rally
South Carolina
21st July 2015

John Kerry:

"He's in a bicycle race. He's seventy-three years old! Seventy-three years old! And I said it the last time I spoke: I swear to you, I will never enter a bicycle race if I'm president. I swear! I swear! He's in a bicycle race! He falls and breaks his leg. This is our chief negotiator. He's walking in and they're looking at him thinking what a schmuck."

Campaign Rally
Iowa
25th August 2015

On MMA fighter Ronda Rousey's support for Bernie Sanders:

"Glad to see that @RondaRousey lost her championship fight last night. Was soundly beaten - not a nice person!"

Twitter
15th November 2015

On Barack Obama:

"Who was it that secretly said to Russian President, 'Tell Vladimir that after the election I'll have more flexibility?'"

Twitter
5th March 2017

"And it's going to get worse, because remember, Obamacare really kicks in in 2016. Obama is going to be out playing golf. He might be on one of my courses. I would invite him, I actually would say. I have the best courses in the world, so I'd say, you what, if he wants to - I have one right next to the White House, right on the Potomac. If he'd like to play, that's fine."

Twitter
Presidential Announcement Speech
16th June 2015

"If Obama resigns from office now, thereby doing a great service to the country, I will give him free lifetime golf at any of my courses!"

Twitter
11th September 2014

"Can you imagine what the outcry would be if @SnoopDogg, failing career and all, had aimed and fired the gun at President Obama? Jail time!"

Twitter
15th March 2017

"122 vicious prisoners, released by the Obama Administration from Gitmo, have returned to the battlefield. Just another terrible decision!"

Twitter
7th March 2017

"Crimea was TAKEN by Russia during the Obama Administration. Was Obama too soft on Russia?"

Twitter
15th February 2017

"Ungrateful TRAITOR Chelsea Manning, who should never have been released from prison, is now calling President Obama a weak leader. Terrible!"

Twitter
26th January 2017

"I don't know Putin, have no deals in Russia, and the haters are going crazy - yet Obama can make a deal with Iran, #1 in terror, no problem!"

Twitter
7th February 2017

"Why is Obama playing basketball today?
That's why our country is in trouble!"

Twitter
6th November 2012

"The way president Obama runs down the
stairs of Air Force 1, hopping & bobbing all
the way, is so inelegant and unpresidential.
Do not fall!"

Twitter
22nd April 2014

"We have a president who doesn't have a
clue. I would say he's incompetent, but I don't
want to do that because that's not nice."

Fox News
6th August 2015

"A fantastic day in D.C. Met with President
Obama for first time. Really good meeting,
great chemistry. Melania liked Mrs. O a lot!"

Twitter
10th November 2016

On Barrack Obama's birth certificate:

"He may have one but there's something on that, maybe religion, maybe it says he is a Muslim. I don't know. Maybe he doesn't want that. Or he may not have one. I will tell you this: if he wasn't born in this country, it's one of the great scams of all time."

March 30th 2011

"An extremely credible source has called my office and told me that Barack Obama's birth certificate is a fraud."

Twitter
6th August 2012

"Obama finally gave his birth certificate and I got such credit for that because I accomplished something that nobody else had accomplished."

Political Rally
Las Vegas
28th April 2011

"President Barack Obama was born in the United States. Period."

Veterans' Rally
Washington DC
16th September 2016

On the wiretapping scandal:

"Terrible! Just found out that Obama had my 'wires tapped' in Trump Tower just before the victory. Nothing found. This is McCarthyism!"

Twitter
4th March 2017

"I'd bet a good lawyer could make a great case out of the fact that President Obama was tapping my phones in October, just prior to Election!"

Twitter
4th March 2017

"How low has President Obama gone to tapp (sic) my phones during the very sacred election process. This is Nixon/Watergate. Bad (or sick) guy!"

Twitter
4th March 2017

When questioned about his wiretapping allegations:

"…and don't forget I say wiretapping, those words were in quotes."

Fox News
15th March 2017

"Wiretapping was in quotes. What I'm talking about is surveillance."

Time Magazine
March 2017

"The real story turns out to be SURVEILLANCE and LEAKING! Find the leakers."

Twitter
2nd April 2017

On Hilary Clinton:

"If Hilary Clinton can't satisfy her husband what makes her think she can satisfy America?"

Twitter
16th April 2015

"People would have been far more forgiving if he'd had an affair with a really beautiful woman of sophistication. Kennedy and Marilyn Monroe were on a different level. Now Clinton can't get into golf clubs in Westchester. A former president begging to get in a golf club. It's unthinkable."

The New York Times
19th September 1999

"She [Hilary Clinton] stays in Trump Tower when she's in New York. Not because of me, but because of somebody else who has an apartment in Trump Tower. At least she has good taste."

CNN
28th November 1999

"I think the only card she has is the women's card. She has got nothing else going. Frankly, if Hillary Clinton were a man, I don't think she would get 5% of the vote. And the beautiful thing is women don't like her, ok?"

Press Conference
New York
26th April 2016

"Why isn't the House Intelligence Committee looking into the Bill & Hillary deal that allowed big Uranium to go to Russia [?]"

Twitter
27th March 2017

"Within ICE [Immigration and Customs Enforcement], I am going to create a new special Deportation Task Force, focused on identifying and quickly removing the most dangerous criminal illegal immigrants in America who have evaded justice just like Hilary Clinton has evaded justice. Ok? Maybe they'll be able to deport her."

Campaign Rally
Phoenix Arizona
31st August 2016

"The result of her misconduct was the release of thousands and thousands of dangerous criminal aliens who should have been sent home to their countries. Instead, we have them all over the place. Probably a couple in this room as a matter of fact, but I hope not."

Campaign Rally
Phoenix Arizona
31st August 2016

"Vladimir Putin said today about Hillary and Dems: 'In my opinion, it is humiliating. One must be able to lose with dignity.' So true!"

Twitter
23rd December 2016

"What are Hillary Clinton's people complaining about with respect to the F.B.I. Based on the information they had she should never have been allowed to run - guilty as hell. They were VERY nice to her. She lost because she campaigned in the wrong states - no enthusiasm!"

Twitter
13th January 2017

"Countless Americans who have died in recent years would be alive today if not for the open border policies of this administration and the administration that causes this horrible, horrible thought process, called Hilary Clinton."

Campaign Rally
Phoenix Arizona
31st August 2016

"This Russian connection non-sense is merely an attempt to cover-up the many mistakes made in Hillary Clinton's losing campaign."

Twitter
15th February 2017

"She promises uncontrolled low-skilled immigration that continues to reduce jobs and wages for American workers, especially African-American and Hispanic workers."

Campaign Rally
Phoenix Arizona
31st August 2016

On Condoleezza Rice:

"I see Condoleezza Rice – she goes on a plane, she gets off a plane, she waves, she goes there to meet some dictator. They talk, she leaves, she waves, the plane takes off. Nothing happens, it's a joke, nothing ever happens."

Hannity's America
January 2007

"Great meeting with a wonderful woman today, former Secretary of State, Condoleezza Rice!"

Twitter
31st March 2017

On Ted Cruz:

"His father was with Lee Harvey Oswald prior to Oswald's being – you know, shot. I mean, the whole thing is ridiculous. What is this, right prior to his being shot, and nobody even brings it up. They don't even talk about that. That was reported, and nobody talks about it."

Fox News
3rd May 2016

On former president Ronal Reagan:

"He is so smooth and so effective a performer that he completely won over the American people. Only now, nearly seven years later, are people beginning to question whether there's anything beneath that smile."

Trump: The Art of the Deal
1987

On Winston Churchill:

"Winston Churchill was an unbelievable
leader. Why? He was born with a speech
impediment. He had all sorts of problems. He
certainly wasn't a handsome man. And, yet,
he was a great leader. Why was he a great
leader? Nobody knows."

Larry King Live
8th October 1999

On Senator John McCain:

"Sen. McCain should not be talking about the
success or failure of a mission to the media.
Only emboldens the enemy! He's been losing
so long he doesn't know how to win anymore,
just look at the mess our country is in -
bogged down in conflict all over the place.
Our hero Ryan died on a winning mission
(according to General Mattis), not a 'failure'.
Time for the U.S. to get smart and start
winning again!"

Twitter
9th February 2017

"He's a war hero? He's a war hero because he was captured? I like people that weren't captured."

Iowa
18th July 2015

On former Ku Klux Klan grand wizard David Duke:

"Just so you understand, I don't know anything about David Duke, OK? I don't know anything about what you're even talking about with white supremacy or white supremacists. So I don't know. I don't know, did he endorse me, or what's going on? Because I know nothing about David Duke; I know nothing about white supremacists."

CNN
28th February 2016

"The Reform Party now includes a Klansman, Mr. Duke, a neo-Nazi, Mr. [Patrick] Buchanan, and a communist, Ms. [Lenora] Fulani. This is not company I wish to keep."

Statement dismissing the Reform Party's nomination for president
13th February 2000

"Well, you've got David Duke just joined
[the Reform Party] — a bigot, a racist, a
problem. I mean, this is not exactly the people
you want in your party."

NBC
14th February 2000

"I don't need [David Duke's] endorsement; I
certainly wouldn't want his endorsement. I
don't need anyone's endorsement."

Bloomberg
26th August 2015

"I don't know anything about him. Somebody
told me yesterday, whoever he is, he did
endorse me. Actually I don't think it was an
endorsement. He said I was absolutely the
best of all of the candidates."

Bloomberg
26th August 2015

When asked if he renounced the support of white supremacist groups:

"Of course, I am. I mean, there's nobody that's done so much for equality as I have. You take a look at Palm Beach, Florida, I built the Mar-a-Lago Club, totally open to everybody; a club that frankly set a new standard in clubs and a new standard in Palm Beach and I've gotten great credit for it. That is totally open to everybody. So, of course, I am."

ABC
1st March 2016

On WikiLeaks:

"This just came out. WikiLeaks! I love WikiLeaks!"

Campaign Rally
Wilkes-Barre, Pennsylvania
10th October 2016

"Never heard of Wikileaks, never heard of it. When Wikileaks came out, all I was just saying is, "Well, look at all this information here, this is pretty good stuff."

Associated Press
21st April 2017

On Congressman Elijah Cummings:

"He said you will be the greatest president. He said you will be, in front of five, six people, he said you will be the greatest president in the history of this country."

Associated Press
21st April 2017

"I watched him interviewed a week later and it's like he was never in my office."

Associated Press
21st April 2017

International Relations

In which Mr Trump gives us his thoughts on Russia, nuclear holocaust, uranium, Brexit, NATO, and North Korea

"We assembled here today are issuing a new decree to be heard in every city, in every foreign capital, and in every hall of power. From this day forward, a new vision will govern our land. From this day forward, it's going to be only America first, America first.

Inauguration Address
Washington DC
20th January 2017

"We will seek friendship and goodwill with the nations of the world – but we do so with the understanding that it is the right of all nations to put their own interests first. We do not seek to impose our way of life on anyone, but rather to let it shine as an example for everyone to follow."

Inauguration Address
Washington DC
20th January 2017

"The Bible tells us how good and pleasant it is when God's people live together in unity."

Inauguration Address
Washington DC
20th January 2017

"I want to tell the world community that while we will always put America's interests first, we will deal fairly with everyone, with everyone. All people and all other nations. We will seek common ground, not hostility; partnership, not conflict."

Election Victory Speech
New York
9th November 2016

On the military:

"I will find within our military… I will find the General Patton or I will find General MacArthur, I will find the right guy. I will find the guy that's going to take that military and make it really work. Nobody, nobody will be pushing us around."

Presidential Announcement Speech
New York
16th June 2017

"Our military is building and is rapidly becoming stronger than ever before. Frankly, we have no choice!"

Twitter
16th April 2017

"So now ISIS has the oil, and what they don't have, Iran has. And in 19… and I will tell you this, and I said it very strongly, years ago, I said… and I love the military, and I want to have the strongest military that we've ever had, and we need it more now than ever."

Presidential Announcement Speech
New York
16th June 2015

"Even our nuclear arsenal doesn't work. It came out recently they have equipment that is 30 years old. They don't know if it worked. And I thought it was horrible when it was broadcast on television, because boy, does that send signals to Putin and all of the other people that look at us and they say, 'That is a group of people, and that is a nation that truly has no clue.'"

Presidential Announcement Speech
New York
16th June 2015

On the F35 fighter jet:

"The F-35 program and cost is out of control. Billions of dollars can and will be saved on military (and other) purchases after January 20th."

Twitter
12th December 2016

"A little before I took office there was a terrible article about the F-35 fighter jet. It was hundreds of billions of dollars over budget. It was seven years behind schedule. It was a disaster."

Associated Press
21st April 2017

"I saved $725 million on the 90 planes. Just 90. Now there are 3,000 planes that are going to be ordered. On 90 planes I saved $725 million. It's actually a little bit more than that, but it's $725 million... Now if you multiply that times 3,000 planes, you know this is on 90 planes... Now you know that's a saving of billions and billions of dollars, many billions of dollars over the course of — it's between 2,500 and 3,000 planes will be the final order. But this was only 90 of those 2,500 planes."

Associated Press
21st April 2017

On NATO:

"I've developed great relationships with all of these leaders. Nobody's written that. In fact, they said, 'Oh, well, he's not treating them nicely,' because on NATO, I want them to pay up. But I still get along with them great, and they will pay up. In fact, with the Italian prime minister yesterday, you saw, we were joking, 'Come on, you have to pay up, you have to pay up.' He'll pay. He's going to end up paying... But you know, nobody ever asked the question. Nobody asked. Nobody ever asked him to pay up."

Associated Press
21st April 2017

"You know, back when they did NATO there was no such thing as terrorism."

Associated Press
21st April 2017

On overseas aid:

"The US cannot allow Ebola infected people back. People who go to faraway places to help out are great, but must suffer the consequences."

Twitter
2nd September 2014

"Stop the EBOLA patients from entering the U.S. Treat them, at the highest level, over there. THE UNITED STATES HAS ENOUGH PROBLEMS!"

Twitter
August 2014

On the special relationship with the UK:

"Many people would like to see @Nigel_Farage represent Great Britain as their Ambassador to the United States. He would do a great job!"

Twitter
21st November 2016

On Brexit:

"I would say that they're better off without it [the EU], personally, but I'm not making that as a recommendation, I want them to make their own decision."

May 2016
Fox News

"I don't think anybody should listen to me because I haven't really focused on it very much."

Fox Business
22nd June 2016

"I said that in Scotland and in the UK, that was going to happen. I was the one that predicted it. And everybody said, he's wrong, he's wrong."

New York
16th July 2016

Following the March 2017 attack on Westminster Bridge:

"Spoke to U.K. Prime Minister Theresa May today to offer condolences on the terrorist attack in London. She is strong and doing very well."

Twitter
22nd March 2017

"A great American, Kurt Cochran, was killed in the London terror attack. My prayers and condolences are with his family and friends."

Twitter
23rd March 2017

On maintaining a healthy relationship with Russia:

"If he [Vladimir Putin] says great things about me, I'm gonna say great things about him. I've already said he is really very much of a leader. I mean, the man has very strong control over a country. And that's a very different system and I don't happen to like the system. But certainly in that system he's been a leader, far more than our president has been a leader."

NBC
7th September 2016

"Having a good relationship with Russia is a good thing, not a bad thing. Only 'stupid' people, or fools, would think that it is bad! We have enough problems around the world without yet another one. When I am President, Russia will respect us far more than they do now and both countries will, perhaps, work together to solve some of the many great and pressing problems and issues of the WORLD!"

Twitter
7th January 2017

"And I can tell you one thing about a briefing that we're allowed to say, because anybody that ever read the most basic book can say it: nuclear holocaust would be like no other. They're a very powerful nuclear country and so are we. If we have a good relationship with Russia, believe me, that's a good thing, not a bad thing."
White House Press Conference
16th February 2017

"You know what uranium is, right? This thing called nuclear weapons, like lots of things are done with uranium, including some bad things."
White House Press Conference
16th February 2017

"Russia has never tried to use leverage over me. I HAVE NOTHING TO DO WITH RUSSIA - NO DEALS, NO LOANS, NO NOTHING!"
Twitter
11th January 2017

"Things will work out fine between the U.S.A. and Russia. At the right time everyone will come to their senses & there will be lasting peace!"

Twitter
April 13th 2017

On nuclear capability:

"The United States must greatly strengthen and expand its nuclear capability until such time as the world comes to its senses regarding nukes"

Twitter
22nd December 2016

"The @nytimes states today that DJT believes 'more countries should acquire nuclear weapons.' How dishonest are they. I never said this!"

Twitter
13th November 2016

On Germany and Angela Merkel:

"Despite what you have heard from the
FAKE NEWS, I had a GREAT meeting with
German Chancellor Angela Merkel.
Nevertheless, Germany owes vast sums of
money to NATO & the United States must be
paid more for the powerful, and very
expensive, defense it provides to Germany!"

Twitter
18th March 2017

"I'm at odds on, you know, the NATO
payments and I'm at odds on immigration. We
had unbelievable chemistry. And people have
given me credit for having great chemistry
with all of the leaders."

Associated Press
21st April 2017

On the French presidential election:

"Another terrorist attack in Paris. The people
of France will not take much more of this.
Will have a big effect on presidential
election!"

Twitter
21st April 2017

"I am not endorsing her [Marine Le Pen] and I didn't mention her name... I believe whoever is the toughest on radical Islamic terrorism and whoever is the toughest at the borders will do well at the election. I am not saying that person is going to win, she is not even favoured to win, you know. Right now, she is in second place."

Associated Press
21st April 2017

On North Korea:

"North Korea is behaving very badly. They have been 'playing' the United States for years. China has done little to help!"

Twitter
17th March 2017

"China is very much the economic lifeline to North Korea so, while nothing is easy, if they want to solve the North Korean problem, they will"

Twitter
21st April 2017

"North Korea is looking for trouble. If China decides to help, that would be great. If not, we will solve the problem without them! U.S.A."

Twitter
11th April 2017

"I explained to the President of China that a trade deal with the U.S. will be far better for them if they solve the North Korean problem!"

Twitter
11th April 2017

"China has been taking out massive amounts of money & wealth from the U.S. in totally one-sided trade, but won't help with North Korea. Nice!"

Twitter
2nd January 2017

"President Xi, we have a, like, a really great relationship. For me to call him a currency manipulator and then say, 'By the way, I'd like you to solve the North Korean problem,' doesn't work."

Associated Press
21st April 2017

"North Korea just stated that it is in the final stages of developing a nuclear weapon capable of reaching parts of the U.S. It won't happen!"

Twitter
2nd January 2017

"Had a very good call last night with the President of China concerning the menace of North Korea."

Twitter
12th April 2017

"I have great confidence that China will properly deal with North Korea. If they are unable to do so, the U.S., with its allies, will! U.S.A."

Twitter
13th April 2017

"But President Xi, from the time I took office, he has not, they have not been currency manipulators. Because there's a certain respect because he knew I would do something or whatever. But more importantly than him not being a currency manipulator the bigger picture, bigger than even currency manipulation, if he's helping us with North Korea, with nuclear and all of the things that go along with it, who would call, what am I going to do, say, 'By the way, would you help us with North Korea? And also, you're a currency manipulator.' It doesn't work that way."

Associated Press
21st April 2017

"There is a chance that we could end up having a major, major conflict with North Korea. Absolutely. We'd love to solve things diplomatically but it's very difficult. I believe he [the Chinese president] is trying very hard. He certainly doesn't want to see turmoil and death. He doesn't want to see it. He is a good man. He is a very good man and I got to know him very well."

Reuters
27th April 2017

"North Korea disrespected the wishes of China & its highly respected President when it launched, though unsuccessfully, a missile today. Bad!"

Twitter
28th April 2017

On China:

"China steals United States Navy research drone in international waters - rips it out of water and takes it to China in unpresidented [sic] act."

Twitter
17th December 2016

"We should tell China that we don't want the drone they stole back.- let them keep it!"

Twitter
17th December 2016

On Russia:

"Russia – this is fake news put out by the media."

White House Press Conference
16th February 2017

"Russians are playing @CNN and @NBCNews for such fools - funny to watch, they don't have a clue! @FoxNews totally gets it!"

Twitter
30th December 2016

"[Vladimir Putin] is not going into Ukraine, OK, just so you understand. He's not gonna go into Ukraine, all right? You can mark it down. You can put it down."

31st July 2016
(Russia had already annexed the Crimea in 2014)

"For eight years Russia 'ran over' President Obama, got stronger and stronger, picked-off Crimea and added missiles. Weak!"

Twitter
7th March 2017

"@FoxNews 'Outgoing CIA Chief, John Brennan, blasts Pres-Elect Trump on Russia threat. Does not fully understand.' Oh really, couldn't do much worse - just look at Syria (red line), Crimea, Ukraine and the build-up of Russian nukes. Not good! Was this the leaker of Fake News?"

Twitter
15th January 2017

"If Russia, or some other entity, was hacking, why did the White House wait so long to act? Why did they only complain after Hillary lost?"

Twitter
15th December 2016

"Russia, if you're listening, I hope you're able to find the 30,000 emails that are missing. I think you will probably be rewarded mightily by our press."

27th July 2016

"I was shocked to hear [Vladimir Putin] mention the N-word. You know what the N-word is. Number one he doesn't like him [Barack Obama] and number two he doesn't respect him. I think he's going to respect your president if I'm elected and I hope he likes me."

27th July 2016

On Cuba:

"Fidel Castro is dead!"

Twitter
26th November 2016

"If Cuba is unwilling to make a better deal
for the Cuban people, the Cuban/American
people and the U.S. as a whole, I will
terminate deal."

Twitter
28th November 2016

And the Irish…

"Happy Lá Fheile Phadraig to all of my great
Irish friends!"

Twitter
17th March 2017

Immigration

In which Mr Trump clarifies his position on Mexico, Sweden, Syria, and the Great Southern Border Wall

"You wouldn't be hearing about the word immigration if it weren't for Donald Trump. I brought the whole subject up!"

NBC News
8th July 2015

"We will terminate the Obama Administration's deadly, and it is deadly, non-enforcement policies that allow thousands of criminal aliens to freely roam our streets, walk around, do whatever they want to do, crime all over the place."

Campaign Rally
Phoenix Arizona
31st August 2016

"Donald J. Trump is calling for a total and complete shutdown of Muslims entering the United States until our country's representatives can figure out what is going on."

Presidential Campaign Pledge (Later Retracted)
7th December 2015

"I call it extreme vetting, right? Extreme vetting. I want extreme. It's going to be so tough, and if somebody comes in that's fine and they're going to be good. It's extreme… And we will get the right people. An ideological certification to make sure that those we are admitting to our country share our values and love our people."

Campaign Rally
Phoenix Arizona
31st August 2016

"We also have to be honest about the fact that not everyone who seeks to join our country will be able to successfully assimilate. Sometimes it's just not going to work out. It is our right as a sovereign nation to choose immigrants that we think are the likeliest to thrive and flourish and love us."

Campaign Rally
Phoenix Arizona
31st August 2016

"The crackdown on illegal criminals is merely the keeping of my campaign promise. Gang members, drug dealers & others are being removed!"

Twitter
12th February 2017

"According to federal data, there are at least 2 million, 2 million, think of it, criminal aliens now inside of our country. 2 million people criminal aliens. We will begin moving them out day one. As soon as I take office. Day One. In joint operation with local, state and federal law enforcement."

Campaign Rally
Phoenix Arizona
31st August 2016

"We're rounding 'em up in a very humane way, in a very nice way. And they're going to be happy because they want to be legalized. And, by the way, I know it doesn't sound nice. But not everything is nice."

60 Minutes
27th September 2015

"While there are many illegal immigrants in our country who are good people, this doesn't change the fact that most illegal immigrants are lower-skilled workers with less education who compete directly against vulnerable American workers, and that these illegal workers draw much more out from the system than they will ever pay in."

Campaign Rally
Phoenix Arizona
31st August 2016

"Do you believe it? The Obama Administration agreed to take thousands of illegal immigrants from Australia. Why? I will study this dumb deal!"

Twitter
1st February 2017

"The joint statement of former presidential candidates John McCain & Lindsey Graham is wrong - they are sadly weak on immigration. The two senators should focus their energies on ISIS, illegal immigration and border security instead of always looking to start World War III."

Twitter
29th January 2017

"Our country needs strong borders and extreme vetting, NOW. Look what is happening all over Europe and, indeed, the world - a horrible mess!"

Twitter
29th January 2017

"This election, and I believe this, is our last chance to secure the border, stop illegal immigration, and reform our laws to make your life better. I really believe this is it. This is our last time. November 8. You got to get out and vote on November 8."

Campaign Rally
Phoenix Arizona
31st August 2016

On Mexico:

"This is a country where we speak English, not Spanish."

CNN
16th September 2015

"Happy Cinco de Mayo! The best taco bowls are made in Trump Tower Grill. I love Hispanics!"

Twitter

"General Kelly is doing a great job at the border. Numbers are way down. Many are not even trying to come in anymore."

Twitter
26th March 2017

"When Mexico sends its people, they're not sending their best. They're not sending you. They're not sending you. They're sending people that have lots of problems, and they're bringing those problems with us (sic). They're bringing drugs. They're bringing crime. They're rapists. And some, I assume, are good people."

Presidential Announcement Speech
New York
16th June 2015

"Mexico has taken advantage of the U.S. for long enough. Massive trade deficits & little help on the very weak border must change, NOW!"

Twitter
27th January 2017

"I love Mexico. I mean, Mexico, I have thousands of people from Mexico that work for me. Thousands. Hispanics."

The Economist
3rd September 2015

"Our leaders are stupid, our politicians are stupid, and the Mexican government is much sharper, much more cunning. They send the bad ones over because they don't want to pay for them, they don't want to take care of them."

Presidential Debate
6th August 2015

"I have just landed having returned from a very important and special meeting with the President of Mexico – a man I like and respect very much, and a man who truly loves his country. Just like I am a man who loves the United States… We also discussed the great contributions of Mexican-American citizens to our two countries, my love for the people of Mexico, and the close friendship between our two nations."

Campaign Rally
Phoenix Arizona
31st August 2016

On the great border wall:

"Number one. Are you ready? We will build a great wall along the southern border. And Mexico will pay for the wall. One hundred percent. They don't know it yet, but they're going to pay for it. And they're great people and great leaders but they're going to pay for the wall. On day one, we will begin working on intangible, physical, tall, power, beautiful southern border wall."

Campaign Rally
Phoenix Arizona
31st August 2016

"I am reading that the great border WALL will cost more than the government originally thought, but I have not gotten involved in the design or negotiations yet. When I do, just like with the F-35 Fighter Jet or the Air Force One Program, price will come WAY DOWN!"

Twitter
11th February 2017

"I said we need to build a wall and it has to be built quickly. I don't mind having a big, beautiful door in that wall so that people can come into this country legally."

Fox News
6th August 2015

"It will be a real wall. It will be a wall that works. It'll actually be a wall that will look good, believe it or not. Because what they have now is a joke. They're ugly, little, and don't work."

60 Minutes
27th September 2015

"I would build a great wall, and nobody builds walls better than me, believe me, and I'll build them very inexpensively, I will build a great, great wall on our southern border. And I will have Mexico pay for that wall."

Presidential Announcement Speech
New York
16th June 2015

"Dishonest media says Mexico won't be paying for the wall if they pay a little later so the wall can be built more quickly. Media is fake!"

Twitter
8th January 2017

"The dishonest media does not report that any money spent on building the Great Wall (for sake of speed), will be paid back by Mexico later!"

Twitter
6th January 2017

"Eventually, but at a later date so we can get started early, Mexico will be paying, in some form, for the badly needed border wall."

Twitter
23rd April 2017

"The Wall is a very important tool in stopping drugs from pouring into our country and poisoning our youth (and many others)! If the wall is not built, which it will be, the drug situation will NEVER be fixed the way it should be! #BuildTheWall"

Twitter
24th April 2017

"Don't let the fake media tell you that I have changed my position on the WALL. It will get built and help stop drugs, human trafficking etc."

Twitter
25th April 2017

"That wall's getting built, OK? One hundred percent. One hundred percent it's getting built. And it's also getting built for much less money."

Associated Press
21st April 2017

On US District Judge Gonzalo Curiel:

"I've been treated very unfairly by this judge. Now, this judge is of Mexican heritage. I'm building a wall, OK? Im building a wall."

CNN
5th June 2016

On Syria:

"It is not compassionate, but reckless, to allow uncontrolled entry from places where proper vetting cannot occur ... We cannot allow a beachhead of terrorism to form inside America – we cannot allow our nation to become a sanctuary for extremists."

Congressional Speech
Washington DC
28th February 2017

"What I won't do is take in two hundred thousand Syrians who could be ISIS. I have been watching the migration. And I see people. I mean, they're men. They're mostly men, and they're strong men. These are physically young, strong men. They look like prime-time soldiers. Now it's probably not true, but where are the women? So, you ask two things. Number one, why aren't they fighting for their country? And, number two. I don't want these people coming over here."

CBS News
11th October 2015

"This could be the greatest Trojan horse. This could make the Trojan horse look like peanuts if these people turned out to be a lot of ISIS."

CBS News
11th October 2015

"Most incredibly, because to me this is unbelievable, we have no idea who these people are, where they come from. I always say Trojan horse. Watch what is going to happen, folks. It's not going to be pretty."

Campaign Rally
Phoenix Arizona
31st August 2016

On a fictitious event in Sweden:

"You look at what's happening last night in Sweden. Sweden. Who would believe this? Sweden. They took in large numbers. They're having problems like they never thought possible."

Political Rally
18th February 2017

Political Rally
18th February 2017

On being informed that there had been no incident in Sweden the previous evening:

"My statement as to what's happening in Sweden was in reference to a story that was broadcast on @FoxNews concerning immigrants & Sweden."

Twitter
19th February 2017

"Give the public a break - The FAKE NEWS media is trying to say that large scale immigration in Sweden is working out just beautifully. NOT!"

Twitter
20th February 2017

On the travel ban:

"72% of refugees admitted into U.S. (2/3 - 2/11) during COURT BREAKDOWN are from 7 countries: SYRIA, IRAQ, SOMALIA, IRAN, SUDAN, LIBYA & YEMEN"

Twitter
12th February 2017

"Our legal system is broken! '77% of refugees allowed into U.S. since travel reprieve hail from seven suspect countries.' (WT) SO DANGEROUS!"

Twitter
11th February 2017

"Big increase in traffic into our country from certain areas, while our people are far more vulnerable, as we wait for what should be EASY D!"

Twitter
8th February 2017

"The threat from radical Islamic terrorism is very real, just look at what is happening in Europe and the Middle-East. Courts must act fast!"

Twitter
6th February 2017

"I have instructed Homeland Security to check people coming into our country VERY CAREFULLY. The courts are making the job very difficult!"

Twitter
5th February 2017

"Just cannot believe a judge would put our country in such peril. If something happens blame him and court system. People pouring in. Bad!"

Twitter
5th February 2017

"The judge opens up our country to potential terrorists and others that do not have our best interests at heart. Bad people are very happy!"

Twitter
4th February 2017

"Because the ban was lifted by a judge, many very bad and dangerous people may be pouring into our country. A terrible decision"

Twitter
4th February 2017

"What is our country coming to when a judge can halt a Homeland Security travel ban and anyone, even with bad intentions, can come into U.S.?"

Twitter
4th February 2017

"The opinion of this so-called judge, which essentially takes law-enforcement away from our country, is ridiculous and will be overturned!"

Twitter
4th February 2017

"Interesting that certain Middle-Eastern countries agree with the ban. They know if certain people are allowed in it's death & destruction!"

Twitter
4th February 2017

"When a country is no longer able to say who can, and who cannot , come in & out, especially for reasons of safety &.security - big trouble!"

Twitter
4th February 2017

"We must keep "evil" out of our country!"

Twitter
3rd February 2017

"If the ban were announced with a one week notice, the 'bad' would rush into our country during that week. A lot of bad 'dudes' out there!"

Twitter
30th January 2017

"There is nothing nice about searching for terrorists before they can enter our country. This was a big part of my campaign. Study the world!"

Twitter
30th January 2017

Responding to claims that the travel ban imposed by the newly elected Trump administration had caused international chaos, whilst attracting global condemnation:

"We had a very smooth rollout of the travel ban."

White House Press Conference
16th February 2017

"Only 109 people out of 325,000 were detained and held for questioning. Big problems at airports were caused by Delta computer outage, protesters and the tears of Senator Schumer. Secretary Kelly said that all is going well with very few problems. MAKE AMERICA SAFE AGAIN!"

Twitter
30th January 2017

Trade

In which Mr Trump explains the trade deficit, protectionism, and how he intends to deal with America's trade partners

"Every decision on trade, on taxes, on immigration, on foreign affairs, will be made to benefit American workers and American families. We must protect our borders from the ravages of other countries making our products, stealing our companies, and destroying our jobs. Protection will lead to great prosperity and strength."

Inauguration Address
Washington DC
20th January 2017

"Toyota Motor said will build a new plant in Baja, Mexico, to build Corolla cars for U.S. NO WAY! Build plant in U.S. or pay big border tax."

Twitter
5th January 2017

"Who is our chief negotiator? Essentially it is Caroline Kennedy. I mean, give me a break, she doesn't even know she's alive."

The Economist
3rd September 2015

"The U.S. is going to substantially reduce taxes and regulations on businesses, but any business that leaves our country for another country, fires its employees, builds a new factory or plant in the other country, and then thinks it will sell its product back into the U.S. without retribution or consequence, is WRONG! There will be a tax on our soon to be strong border of 35% for these companies wanting to sell their product, cars, A.C. units etc., back across the border. This tax will make leaving financially difficult, but these companies are able to move between all 50 states, with no tax or tariff being charged. Please be forewarned prior to making a very expensive mistake! THE UNITED STATES IS OPEN FOR BUSINESS"

Twitter
4th December 2016

"Countries charge U.S. companies taxes or tariffs while the U.S. charges them nothing or little. We should charge them SAME as they charge us!"

Twitter
3rd February 2017

"We have very stupid people in our country negotiating for us, and we have leaders that don't know what they're doing."

NBC News
8 July 2015

"Free trade can be wonderful if you have smart people, but we have people that are stupid. We have people that aren't smart. And we have people that are controlled by special interests. And it's just not going to work."

Presidential Announcement Speech
New York
16 June 2015

On China:

"Did China ask us if it was OK to devalue their currency (making it hard for our companies to compete), heavily tax our products going into their country (the U.S. doesn't tax them) or to build a massive military complex in the middle of the South China Sea? I don't think so!"

Twitter
4 December 2016

"And they don't talk jobs and they don't talk China. When was the last time you heard China is killing us? They're devaluing their currency to a level that you wouldn't believe. It makes it impossible for our companies to compete, impossible. They're killing us."

Presidential Announcement Speech
New York
16th June 2015

"Why would I call China a currency manipulator when they are working with us on the North Korean problem? We will see what happens!"

Twitter
16th April 2017

"People say, 'Oh, you don't like China.' No, I love them. But their leaders are much smarter than our leaders. It's like take the New England Patriots and Tom Brady, and have them play your high school football team. That's the difference between China's leaders and our leaders."

Presidential Announcement Speech
New York
16th June 2015

When was the last time anybody saw us beating, let's say, China in a trade deal? They kill us. I beat China all the time. All the time."

Presidential Announcement Speech
New York
16th June 2015

"Hey, I'm not saying they're stupid. I like China. I sell apartments for... I just sold an apartment for $15 million to somebody from China. Am I supposed to dislike them? I own a big chunk of the Bank of America Building at 1290 Avenue of the Americas that I got from China in a war. Very valuable.
I love China. The biggest bank in the world is from China. You know where their United States headquarters is located? In this building, in Trump Tower. I love China."

Presidential Announcement Speech
New York
16th June 2015

"First of all, I love China. The people are great. They buy my apartments for $50 million all the time. How could I dislike them, right?"

Political Rally
Virginia
14th October 2015

On the April 2017 Official State Visit of Chinese President Xi Jinping:

"The meeting next week with China will be a very difficult one in that we can no longer have massive trade deficits and job losses. American companies must be prepared to look at other alternatives."

Twitter
30th March 2017

"It was a great honor to have President Xi Jinping and Madame Peng Liyuan of China as our guests in the United States. Tremendous goodwill and friendship was formed, but only time will tell on trade."

Twitter
8th April 2017

"I've had cases where the gentleman from China, Ma, Jack Ma (chairman of Alibaba Group), he comes up, he says, 'Only because of you am I making this massive investment.' Intel, only because of you... The press never writes that."

Associated Press
21st April 2017

On Japan:

"Masa (SoftBank) of Japan has agreed to invest $50 billion in the U.S. toward businesses and 50,000 new jobs. Masa said he would never do this had we (Trump) not won the election!"

Twitter
6th December 2016

"After two days of very productive talks, Prime Minister Abe is heading back to Japan."

Twitter
12th February 2017

"When did we beat Japan at anything?"

Presidential Announcement Speech
New York
16th June 2015

On Mexico:

"Rexnord of Indiana is moving to Mexico and rather viciously firing all of its 300 workers. This is happening all over our country. No more!"

Twitter
2nd December 2016

"The U.S. has a 60 billion dollar trade deficit with Mexico. It has been a one-sided deal from the beginning of NAFTA with massive numbers of jobs and companies lost. If Mexico is unwilling to pay for the badly needed wall, then it would be better to cancel the upcoming meeting."

Twitter
26th January 2017

"General Motors is sending Mexican made model of Chevy Cruze to U.S. car dealers tax free across border. Make in U.S.A. or pay big border tax!"

Twitter
3rd January 2017

On Taiwan:

"The President of Taiwan CALLED ME today to wish me congratulations on winning the Presidency. Thank you!"

Twitter
2nd December 2016

"Interesting how the U.S. sells Taiwan billions of dollars of military equipment but I should not accept a congratulatory call."

Twitter
2nd December 2016

Gender Issues

In which Mr Trump provides an insight into women, romance, sex and homosexuality

On women:

"I will be phenomenal to the women. I mean, I want to help women."

CBS News
9th August 2015

"I cherish women. I want to help women. I'm going to be able to do things for women that no other candidate would be able to do."

CNN
9th August 2015

"I will take care of women. I respect women. I will take care of women."

CNN
16th September 2015

"Women are much tougher and more calculating than men. I relate better to women."

The New York Times
19th September 1999

On women in the workplace:

"I have tremendous respect for women and the many roles they serve that are vital to the fabric of our society and our economy."

Twitter
8th March 2017

"I have really given a lot of women great opportunity. Unfortunately, after they are a star, the fun is over for me."

ABC News
10th March 1994

"She's not giving me 100 percent. She's giving me 84 percent, and 16 percent is going toward taking care of children."

Time Magazine
23rd May 2011

On claims of sexual assault being made against him:

"Believe me, she would not be my first choice, that I can tell you."

14th October 2016

"I didn't even apologize to my wife who is sitting right here because I didn't do anything. I didn't know any of these women. I didn't see these women. It was all lies and it was fiction."

Election Debate
19th October 2016

On being accused of making sexist remarks:

"You know I'm automatically attracted to beautiful — I just start kissing them. It's like a magnet. Just kiss. I don't even wait. And when you're a star, they let you do it. You can do anything. Grab them by the p**sy. You can do anything."

Access Hollywood
2005

"This was locker room banter, a private conversation that took place many years ago. Bill Clinton has said far worse to me on the golf course – not even close. I apologize if anyone was offended."

On the wearing of burqas:

"You don't have to put on makeup. Look at how beautiful everyone looks. Wouldn't it be easier? I'm ready darling, let's go."

Campaign Rally
New Hampshire
28th October 2015

On romance:

"Certain guys tell me they want women of substance, not beautiful models. It just means they can't get beautiful models."

The New York Times
19th September 1999

"When a man leaves a woman, especially when it was perceived that he has left for a piece of ass. A good one! There are fifty percent of the population who will love the woman who was left."

Vanity Fair
September 1990

On homosexuality:

"It's like in golf…A lot of people…I don't want this to sound trivial…but a lot of people are switching to these really long putters, very unattractive…It's weird. You see these great players with these really long putters, because they can't sink three footers anymore. And, I hate it. I am a traditionalist. I have so many fabulous friends who happen to be gay, but I am a traditionalist."

The New York Times
1st May 2011

"I know politicians who love women who don't even want to be known for that because they might lose the gay vote."

Playboy Magazine
March 1990

"The LGBT community, the gay community, the lesbian community — they are so much in favor of what I've been saying over the last three or four days. Ask the gays what they think and what they do, in, not only Saudi Arabia, but many of these countries, and then you tell me — who's your friend, Donald Trump or Hillary Clinton?"

15th June 2016

The Middle-East

**In which Mr Trump sheds more light on the US relationship
with Iraq, Iran, Syria, Israel and the war on terror**

On Iraq:

"We spent $2 trillion in Iraq, $2 trillion. We
lost thousands of lives, thousands in Iraq. We
have wounded soldiers, who I love, I love-
they're great - all over the place, thousands
and thousands of wounded soldiers."

Presidential Announcement Speech
New York
16th June 2015

"What was the purpose of this whole thing?
Hundreds and hundreds of young people
killed. And what about the people coming
back with no arms and legs? Not to mention
the other side. All those Iraqi kids who've
been blown to pieces."

Esquire Magazine
August 2004

"If you look at Saddam Hussein, he killed
terrorists. I'm not saying he was an angel, but
this guy killed terrorists."

CNBC
2006

"Saddam Hussein is gonna be like a nice guy compared to the one who's taking over Iraq. Somebody will take over Iraq, whether we're there or not."

CNBC
2006

You have Iran…is going to take over Iraq. I called that many years ago on your show. I said, we should have never gone into Iraq, which I should be given a little credit for vision."

The O'Reilly Factor
28th September 2014

"How about bringing baskets of money into Iraq? I want to know -- who were the soldiers who had that job? I want to know who were the soldiers that had that job, 'cause I think they're living well right now, whoever they may be."

14th June 2016

"And every time we give Iraq equipment, the first time a bullet goes off in the air, they leave it. Last week, I read 2,300 Humvees - these are big vehicles - were left behind for the enemy. 2,000? You would say maybe two, maybe four? 2,300 sophisticated vehicles, they ran, and the enemy took them."

Presidential Announcement Speech
New York
16th June 2015

On Israel:

"The big loss yesterday for Israel in the United Nations will make it much harder to negotiate peace. Too bad, but we will get it done anyway!"

Twitter
24th December 2016

"We cannot continue to let Israel be treated with such total disdain and disrespect. They used to have a great friend in the U.S., but not anymore. The beginning of the end was the horrible Iran deal, and now this (U.N.)! Stay strong Israel, January 20th is fast approaching!"

Twitter
28th December 2016

On the Iraq/Iran war:

"Iraq and Iran were very similar militarily, and they'd fight, fight, fight, and then they'd rest. They'd fight, fight, fight, and then Saddam Hussein would do the gas, and somebody else would do something else, and they'd rest."

Campaign Rally
Virginia Beach
6th September 2016

On Iran

"Iran is playing with fire - they don't appreciate how 'kind' President Obama was to them. Not me!"

Twitter
3rd February 2017

"Iran was on its last legs and ready to collapse until the U.S. came along and gave it a life-line in the form of the Iran Deal: $150 billion"

Twitter
2nd February 2017

"When Iran, when they circle our beautiful destroyers with their little boats, and they make gestures at our people that they shouldn't be allowed to make, they will be shot out of the water."

Campaign Rally
Pensacola, Florida
9th September 2016

"Iran has been formally PUT ON NOTICE for firing a ballistic missile. Should have been thankful for the terrible deal the U.S. made with them!"

Twitter
2nd February 2017

On Saudi Arabia

"Saudi Arabia, they make $1 billion a day. $1 billion a day. I love the Saudis. Many are in this building [Trump Tower]. They make a billion dollars a day. Whenever they have problems, we send over the ships. We say 'we're gonna protect.' What are we doing? They've got nothing but money. If the right person asked them, they'd pay a fortune. They wouldn't be there except for us."

Presidential Announcement Speech
New York
16th June 2015

On Egypt:

"I dealt with Gaddafi. I rented him a piece of land. He paid me more for one night than the land was worth for the whole year, or for two years, and then I didn't let him use the land. That's what we should be doing. I don't want to use the word 'screwed', but I screwed him."

Fox News
21st April 2011

Following a US attack on a Syrian Airbase in April 2017:

"The reason you don't generally hit runways is that they are easy and inexpensive to quickly fix (fill in and top)!"

Twitter
8th April 2017

"Congratulations to our great military men and women for representing the United States, and the world, so well in the Syria attack."

Twitter
8th April 2017

"When it came time to, as an example, send out the 59 missiles, the Tomahawks in Syria. I'm saying to myself, 'You know, this is more than just like, 79 [sic] missiles. This is death that's involved,' because people could have been killed."

Associated Press
21st April 2017

On Islamic Terrorism:

"Today there were terror attacks in Turkey, Switzerland and Germany - and it is only getting worse. The civilized world must change thinking!"

Twitter
19th December 2016

"A new radical Islamic terrorist has just attacked in Louvre Museum in Paris. Tourists were locked down. France on edge again. GET SMART U.S."

Twitter
3rd February 2017

"Appreciate the congrats for being right on radical Islamic terrorism, I don't want congrats, I want toughness & vigilance. We must be smart!"

12th June 2016

"ISIS is taking credit for the terrible stabbing attack at Ohio State University by a Somali refugee who should not have been in our country."

Twitter
30th November 2016

"The terrorist who killed so many people in Germany said just before crime, 'by God's will we will slaughter you pigs, I swear, we will slaughter you.' This is a purely religious threat, which turned into reality. Such hatred! When will the U.S., and all countries, fight back?"

Twitter
23rd December 2016

"When you see the other side chopping off heads, waterboarding doesn't sound very severe."

ABC News
2nd August 2016

"They just built a hotel in Syria. Can you believe this? They built a hotel. When I have to build a hotel, I pay interest. They don't have to pay interest, because they took the oil that, when we left Iraq, I said we should've taken."

Presidential Announcement Speech
New York
16th June 2015

"You take the oil. It's simple. You take the oil. There are certain areas which ISIS has the oil and you take the oil. You keep it. You just go in and take it."

The Economist
3rd September 2015

"I have an absolute way of defeating ISIS, and it would be decisive and quick and it would be very beautiful."

The Des Moines Register
2nd June 2015

"I think ISIS, what they did, was unbelievable. What they did with James Foley and with the cutting off of heads of everybody. I mean these people are totally a disaster."

CBS News
27th September 2015

"If you look at Syria, Russia wants to get rid of ISIS. We want to get rid of ISIS. Maybe let Russia do it. Let them get rid of ISIS. What the hell do we care?"

CBS News
27th September 2015

"We are still fighting Mosul. You know why? Because they were prepared. If we would have gone in and just done it, it would have been over three months ago."

Associated Press
21st April 2017

"There should be no further releases from Gitmo. These are extremely dangerous people and should not be allowed back onto the battlefield."

Twitter
3rd January 2017

On the integrity of Trump Tower during the 9/11 attacks:

"40 Wall Street actually was the second-tallest building in downtown Manhattan, and it was actually, before the World Trade Center, was the tallest—and then, when they built the World Trade Center, it became known as the second-tallest. And now it's the tallest."

Radio WWOR
11th September 2001

"I wrote this out, and it's very close to my heart. Because I was down there and I watched our police and our firemen down at 7/11 (sic), down at the World Trade Center right after it came down. And I saw the greatest people I've ever seen in action."

Campaign Rally
Buffalo, New York
18th April 2016

Environmental Issues

In which Mr Trump expresses his opinions on matters concerning global warming and climate change

On the environment:

"We'll be fine with the environment. We can leave a little bit, but you can't destroy business."

Fox News
18th October 2015

"I am committed to keeping our air and water clean but always remember that economic growth enhances environmental protection. Jobs matter!"

Twitter
22nd April 2017

"Today on Earth Day, we celebrate our beautiful forests, lakes and land. We stand committed to preserving the natural beauty of our nation."

Twitter
22nd April 2017

On Global Warming:

"It's really cold outside, they are calling it a major freeze, weeks ahead of normal. Man, we could use a big fat dose of global warming!"

Twitter
19th October 2015

"NBC News just called it the great freeze-coldest weather in years. Is our country still spending money on the GLOBAL WARMING HOAX?"

Twitter
25th January 2014

"This very expensive GLOBAL WARMING bullshit has got to stop. Our planet is freezing, record low temps, and our GW scientists are stuck in ice."

Twitter
1st January 2014

"The concept of global warming was created by and for the Chinese in order to make US manufacturing non-competitive."

Twitter
6th October 2012

The Media

In which Mr Trump elucidates on television, the press,
celebrity culture, fake news and Rosie O'Donnel

"Rupert Murdoch is a great guy who likes me
much better as a very successful candidate
than he ever did as a very successful
developer!"

Twitter
9th January 2017

"Has anyone looked at the really poor
numbers of @VanityFair Magazine. Way
down, big trouble, dead! Graydon Carter, no
talent, will be out!"

Twitter
15th December 2016

"No matter how much I accomplish during
the ridiculous standard of the first 100 days,
& it has been a lot (including S.C.), media
will kill!"

Twitter
21st April 2017

"Before I, or anyone, saw the classified and/or highly confidential hacking intelligence report, it was leaked out to @NBCNews. So serious!"

Twitter
8th January 2017

"As you know, I have a running war with the media. They are among the most dishonest human beings on Earth. They sort of made it sound like I had a 'feud' with the intelligence community. Nonsense, it is exactly the opposite, and they understand that too."

Press Conference
CIA Headquarters, Virginia
21st January 2017

"The media has not reported that the National Debt in my first month went down by $12 billion vs a $200 billion increase in Obama first mo."

Twitter
25th February 2017

Arnold Schwarzenegger/*The Apprentice*

"Reports by @CNN that I will be working on
The Apprentice during my Presidency, even
part time, are ridiculous & untrue - FAKE
NEWS!"

Twitter
10th December 2016

"I have NOTHING to do with *The
Apprentice* except for fact that I conceived it
with Mark B & have a big stake in it. Will
devote ZERO TIME!"

Twitter
10th December 2016

"Arnold Schwarzenegger isn't voluntarily
leaving *The Apprentice*, he was fired by his
bad (pathetic) ratings, not by me. Sad end to
great show"

Twitter
4th March 2017

"Yes, Arnold Schwarzenegger did a really
bad job as Governor of California and even
worse on *The Apprentice*...but at least he tried
hard!"

Twitter
3rd February 2017

"Wow, the ratings are in and Arnold Schwarzenegger got 'swamped' (or destroyed) by comparison to the ratings machine, DJT. So much for being a movie star-and that was season 1 compared to season 14. Now compare him to my season 1. But who cares, he supported Kasich & Hillary"

Twitter
6th January2017

On Fake News:

"Just watched @NBCNightlyNews - So biased, inaccurate and bad, point after point. Just can't get much worse, although @CNN is right up there!"

Twitter
11th December 2016

"I win an election easily, a great 'movement' is verified, and crooked opponents try to belittle our victory with FAKE NEWS. A sorry state!"

Twitter
11th January 2017

"We had a great News Conference at Trump Tower today. A couple of FAKE NEWS organizations were there but the people truly get what's going on"

Twitter
11th January 2017

"CNN is in a total meltdown with their FAKE NEWS because their ratings are tanking since election and their credibility will soon be gone!"

Twitter
12th January 2017

"Congratulations to @FoxNews for being number one in inauguration ratings. They were many times higher than FAKE NEWS @CNN - public is smart!"

Twitter
24th January 2017

"Any negative polls are fake news, just like the CNN, ABC, NBC polls in the election. Sorry, people want border security and extreme vetting."

Twitter
6th February 2017

"I call my own shots, largely based on an accumulation of data, and everyone knows it. Some FAKE NEWS media, in order to marginalize, lies!"

Twitter
6th February 2017

"Why doesn't Fake News talk about : [Democratic Party Campaign Chairman John] Podesta ties to Russia as covered by @FoxNews or money from Russia to Clinton - sale of Uranium?"

Twitter
28th March 2017

"It is the same Fake News Media that said there is 'no path to victory for Trump' that is now pushing the phony Russia story. A total scam!"

Twitter
1st April 2017

"When will Sleepy Eyes Chuck Todd and @NBCNews start talking about the Obama SURVEILLANCE SCANDAL and stop with the Fake Trump/Russia story?"

Twitter
1st April 2017

"Just watched the totally biased and fake news reports of the so-called Russia story on NBC and ABC. Such dishonesty!"

Twitter
23rd March 2017

"Just heard Fake News CNN is doing polls again despite the fact that their election polls were a WAY OFF disaster. Much higher ratings at Fox"

Twitter
20th March 2017

"Does anybody really believe that a reporter, who nobody ever heard of, 'went to his mailbox' and found my tax returns? @NBCNews FAKE NEWS!"

Twitter
15th March 2017

"Don't let the FAKE NEWS tell you that there is big infighting in the Trump Admin. We are getting along great, and getting major things done!"

Twitter
7th March 2017

"Russia talk is FAKE NEWS put out by the Dems, and played up by the media, in order to mask the big election defeat and the illegal leaks!"

Twitter
26th February 2017

"FAKE NEWS media knowingly doesn't tell the truth. A great danger to our country. The failing @nytimes has become a joke. Likewise @CNN. Sad!"

Twitter
24th February 2017

"Don't believe the main stream (fake news) media. The White House is running VERY WELL. I inherited a MESS and am in the process of fixing it."

Twitter
18th February 2017

"The FAKE NEWS media (failing @nytimes, @NBCNews, @ABC, @CBS, @CNN) is not my enemy, it is the enemy of the American People!"

Twitter
17th February 2017

"The Democrats had to come up with a story as to why they lost the election, and so badly (306), so they made up a story - RUSSIA. Fake news!"

Twitter
16th February 2017

"FAKE NEWS media, which makes up stories and 'sources', is far more effective than the discredited Democrats - but they are fading fast!"

Twitter
16th February 2017

"The fake news media is going crazy with their conspiracy theories and blind hatred. @MSNBC & @CNN are unwatchable. @foxandfriends is great!"

Twitter
15th February2017

"Just leaving Florida. Big crowds of enthusiastic supporters lining the road that the FAKE NEWS media refuses to mention. Very dishonest!"

Twitter
12th February 2017

"While on FAKE NEWS @CNN, Bernie
Sanders was cut off for using the term fake
news to describe the network. They said
technical difficulties!"

Twitter
12th February 2017

"Thank you to Prime Minister of Australia
for telling the truth about our very civil
conversation that FAKE NEWS media lied
about. Very nice!"

Twitter
3rd February 2017

"The same people who did the phony election
polls, and were so wrong, are now doing
approval rating polls. They are rigged just like
before."

Twitter
17th January 2017

"New polls out today are very good
considering that much of the media is FAKE
and almost always negative. Would still beat
Hillary in popular vote."

Twitter
23rd April 2017

"I have learned one thing, because I get treated very unfairly, that's what I call it, the fake media. And the fake media is not all of the media. You know they tried to say that the fake media was all the, no. The fake media is some of you. I could tell you who it is, 100 percent. Sometimes you're fake, but — but the fake media is some of the media. It bears no relationship to the truth. It's not that Fox treats me well, it's that Fox is the most accurate."

Associated Press
21st April 2017

On the New York Times:

"The failing @nytimes just announced that complaints about them are at a 15 year high. I can fully understand that - but why announce?"

Twitter
22nd November 2016

"I cancelled today's meeting with the failing @nytimes when the terms and conditions of the meeting were changed at the last moment. Not nice"

Twitter
22nd November 2016

"Perhaps a new meeting will be set up with the @nytimes. In the meantime they continue to cover me inaccurately and with a nasty tone!"

Twitter
22nd November 2016

"The failing @nytimes was forced to apologize to its subscribers for the poor reporting it did on my election win. Now they are worse!"

Twitter
6th February 2017

"The failing @nytimes writes total fiction concerning me. They have gotten it wrong for two years, and now are making up stories & sources!"

Twitter
6th February 2017

"The failing @nytimes has disgraced the media world. Gotten me wrong for two solid years. Change libel laws?"

Twitter
30th March 2017

"Remember when the failing @nytimes apologized to its subscribers, right after the election, because their coverage was so wrong. Now worse!"

Twitter
29th March 2017

"The failing @NYTimes would do much better if they were honest!"

Twitter
28th March 2017

"For first time the failing @nytimes will take an ad (a bad one) to help save its failing reputation. Try reporting accurately & fairly!"

Twitter
26th February 2017

"Leaking, and even illegal classified leaking, has been a big problem in Washington for years. Failing @nytimes (and others) must apologize!"

Twitter
16th February 2017

"The failing @nytimes does major FAKE NEWS China story saying "Mr.Xi has not spoken to Mr. Trump since Nov.14." We spoke at length yesterday!"

Twitter
10th February 2017

"After being forced to apologize for its bad and inaccurate coverage of me after winning the election, the FAKE NEWS @nytimes is still lost!"

Twitter
4th February 2017

"Somebody with aptitude and conviction should buy the FAKE NEWS and failing @nytimes and either run it correctly or let it fold with dignity!"

Twitter
29th January 2017

"The failing @nytimes has been wrong about me from the very beginning. Said I would lose the primaries, then the general election. FAKE NEWS!"

Twitter
28th January 2017

"The coverage about me in the @nytimes and the @washingtonpost gas been so false and angry that the times actually apologized to its dwindling subscribers and readers. They got me wrong right from the beginning and still have not changed course, and never will. DISHONEST"

Twitter
28th January 2017

"Failing @nytimes, which has been calling me wrong for two years, just got caught in a big lie concerning New England Patriots visit to W.H. [The White House]"

Twitter
20th April 2017

On poor writing:

"They don't write good. They have people over there, like Maggie Haberman and others, they don't — they don't write good. They don't know how to write good."

Fox News
1st August 2016

On an alleged assault by one of his staff on a reporter:

"She had a pen in her hand, which Secret Service is not liking because they don't know what it is, whether it's a little bomb."

CNN
29th March 2016

On CNN:

".@CNN is so embarrassed by their total (100%) support of Hillary Clinton, and yet her loss in a landslide, that they don't know what to do."

Twitter
28th November 2016

"@CNN There is NO QUESTION THAT #voterfraud did take place, and in favor of #CorruptHillary !"

Twitter
28th November 2016

"@Filibuster: @jeffzeleny Pathetic - you have no sufficient evidence that Donald Trump did not suffer from voter fraud, shame! Bad reporter."

Twitter

"@jeffzeleny just another generic CNN part time wannabe journalist! @CNN still doesn't get it. They will never learn!"

Twitter
28th November 2016

"@jeffzeleny what PROOF do u have DonaldTrump did not suffer from millions of FRAUD votes? Journalist? Do your job! @CNN"

Twitter
28th November 2016

On the press:

"You have, I'd say, 10 to 15 to 20 percent who are truly bad people. They're dishonest, they're horrible human beings. They know…it's not a question of being lazy or anything…they actually go out of their way to write false stories."

Campaign Rally
Virginia
14th October 2015

"It is amazing how rude much of the media is to my very hard working representatives. Be nice, you will do much better!"

Twitter
13th March 2017

"The point is that if you are a little different, or a little outrageous, or if you do things that are bold and controversial, the press is going to write about you."

Trump: The Art of the Deal
1987

"If the people of our great country could only see how viciously and inaccurately my administration is covered by certain media!"

Twitter
29th March 2017

"You know, look, I'm on a lot of covers. I think maybe more than almost any supermodel. I think more than any supermodel. But in a way that is a sign of respect, people are respecting what you are doing."

CBS News
27th September 2015

"If the press would cover me accurately &
honorably, I would have far less reason to
'tweet'. Sadly, I don't know if that will ever
happen!"

Twitter
5th December 2016

"I will not be attending the White House
Correspondents' Association Dinner this year.
Please wish everyone well and have a great
evening!"

Twitter
25th February 2017

On Arianna Huffington of the Huffington Post:

"@ariannahuff is unattractive both inside and
out. I fully understand why her former
husband left her for a man. He made a good
decision."

Twitter
28th August 2012

On celebrities and celebrity romance:

"Robert Pattinson should not take back Kristen Stewart. She cheated on him like a dog & will do it again. Just watch. He can do much better!"

Twitter
18th October 2012

"Everyone knows I am right that Robert Pattinson should dump Kristen Stewart. In a couple of years, he will thank me. Be smart, Robert."

Twitter
23rd October 2012

"Katy [Perry], what the hell were you thinking when you married loser Russell Brand. There is a guy who has got nothing going, a waste!"

Twitter
17th October 2014

"Cher is somewhat of a loser. She's lonely. She's unhappy. She's very miserable."

Fox News
14th May 2012

"While Bette Midler is an extremely unattractive woman, I refuse to say that because I always insist on being politically correct."

Twitter
28th October 2012

On Rosie O'Donnell:

"Rosie's a person who's very lucky to have her girlfriend. And she better be careful, or I'll send one of my friends over to pick up her girlfriend. Why would she stay with Rosie if she had another choice?"

Entertainment Tonight
21st December 2006

"Well, Rosie O'Donnell's disgusting, both inside and out. You take a look at her, she's a slob. She talks like a truck driver."

Entertainment Tonight
21st December 2006

"I loved it. I gloat over it. I think it's wonderful, because I like to see bad people fail. Rosie failed? I'm happy about it."

Entertainment Tonight
21st December 2006

"If I were running *The View*, I'd fire Rosie. I mean, I'd look at her right in that fat, ugly face of hers and say, 'Rosie, you're fired.' We're all a little chubby, but Rosie's just worse than most of us."

Entertainment Tonight
21st December 2006

On friends in the media:

"All the haters and losers must admit that, unlike others, I never attacked dopey Jon Stewart for his phony last name. Would never do that!"

Twitter
30th May 2015

"Jay Leno and his people are constantly calling me to go on his show. My answer is always no because his show sucks. They love my ratings!"

Twitter
5th September 2013

"What is it about me that gets Larry King his highest ratings?"

TrumpNation: The Art of Being The Donald
2005

To Larry King:

"Do you mind if I sit back a little bit?
Because your breath is very bad. It really is.
Has this ever been told to you before?"

Larry King Live
15th April 1989

On the Oscars:

"The Oscars are a sad joke, very much like
our president. So many things are wrong!"

Twitter
23rd February 2015

On Meryl Streep:

"Meryl Streep, one of the most over-rated
actresses in Hollywood, doesn't know me but
attacked last night at the Golden Globes. She
is a Hillary flunky who lost big. For the 100th
time, I never 'mocked' a disabled reporter
(would never do that) but simply showed him
'groveling' when he totally changed a 16 year
old story that he had written in order to make
me look bad. Just more very dishonest
media!"

Twitter
9th January 2017

Domestic Issues

In which Mr Trump discusses race relations, crime, the unions and making America great again

"And whether a child is born in the urban sprawl of Detroit or the windswept plains of Nebraska, they look up at the same night sky, they fill their heart with the same dreams, and they are infused with the breath of life by the same almighty Creator."

Inauguration Address
Washington DC
20th January 2017

"No matter what you do, guns, no guns, it doesn't matter. You have people that are mentally ill. And they're gonna come through the cracks. And they're going to do things that people will not even believe are possible."

NBC News
4th October 2015

"Drugs are becoming cheaper than candy bars."

White House Press Conference
16th February 2017

"For many years our country has been divided, angry and untrusting. Many say it will never change, the hatred is too deep. IT WILL CHANGE!!!!"

Twitter
15th January 2017

"For too many of our citizens, a different reality exists: mothers and children trapped in poverty in our inner cities; rusted-out factories scattered like tombstones across the landscape of our nation; an education system, flush with cash, but which leaves our young and beautiful students deprived of all knowledge; and the crime and the gangs and the drugs that have stolen too many lives and robbed our country of so much unrealized potential. This American carnage stops right here and stops right now."

Inauguration Address
Washington DC
20th January 2017

On Race:

"Look at my African American over here!"

Campaign Rally
3rd June 2016

"I have a great relationship with the blacks. I've always had a great relationship with the blacks."

Albany Talk Radio
14th April 2011

"Sadly, because president Obama has done such a poor job as president, you won't see another black president for generations."

Twitter
25th November 2014

"Our great African American President hasn't exactly had a positive impact on the thugs who are so happily and openly destroying Baltimore."

Twitter
28th April 2015

"I have a great relationship with African Americans, as you possibly have heard. I just have great respect for them. And they like me. I like them."

CNN
23rd July 2015

"What do you have to lose by trying something new like Trump? What do you have to lose? You're living in poverty; your schools are no good; you have no jobs; 58 percent of your youth is unemployed. What the hell do you have to lose? At the end of four years, I guarantee you that I will get 95 percent of the African-American vote."

19th August 2016

"Education is the civil rights issue of our time."

Congressional Speech
Washington DC
28th February 2017

On shutting down mosques:

"Well I would hate to do it but it's something you're going to have to strongly consider. Some of the absolute hatred is coming from these areas. The hatred is incredible. It's embedded. The hatred is beyond belief. The hatred is greater than anybody understands."

13th November 2015

On Congressman John Lewis:

"Congressman John Lewis should finally focus on the burning and crime infested inner-cities of the U.S. I can use all the help I can get!"

Twitter
14th January 2017

"Congressman John Lewis should spend more time on fixing and helping his district, which is in horrible shape and falling apart (not to mention crime infested) rather than falsely complaining about the election results. All talk, talk, talk - no action or results. Sad!"

Twitter
14th January 2017

On Chicago:

"Chicago murder rate is record setting - 4,331 shooting victims with 762 murders in 2016. If Mayor can't do it he must ask for Federal help!"

Twitter
2nd January 2017

"If Chicago doesn't fix the horrible 'carnage' going on, 228 shootings in 2017 with 42 killings (up 24% from 2016), I will send in the Feds!"

Twitter
24th January 2017

"Seven people shot and killed yesterday in Chicago. What is going on there - totally out of control. Chicago needs help!"

Twitter
23rd February 2017

"Dwyane Wade's cousin was just shot and killed walking her baby in Chicago. Just what I have been saying. African-Americans will VOTE TRUMP!"

Twitter
27th August 2016

On anti-Trump protests:

"The so-called angry crowds in home districts of some Republicans are actually, in numerous cases, planned out by liberal activists. Sad!"

Twitter
21st February 2017

"Professional anarchists, thugs and paid protesters are proving the point of the millions of people who voted to MAKE AMERICA GREAT AGAIN!"

Twitter
3rd February 2017

"Peaceful protests are a hallmark of our democracy. Even if I don't always agree, I recognize the rights of people to express their views."

Twitter
22nd January 2017

"Watched protests yesterday but was under the impression that we just had an election! Why didn't these people vote? Celebs hurt cause badly."

Twitter
22nd January 2017

"Maybe the millions of people who voted to MAKE AMERICA GREAT AGAIN should have their own rally. It would be the biggest of them all!"

Twitter

"Love the fact that the small groups of protesters last night have passion for our great country. We will all come together and be proud!"

Twitter
11th November 2016

"Just had a very open and successful presidential election. Now professional protesters, incited by the media, are protesting. Very unfair!"

Twitter
10th November 2016

"Someone should look into who paid for the small organized rallies yesterday. The election is over!"

Twitter
16th April 2017

On making America great again:

"We're like the big bully that keeps getting beat up. You ever see that? The big bully that keeps getting beat up."

Campaign Rally
Phoenix Arizona
31st August 2016

"…today we are not merely transferring power from one administration to the other, but from Washington, D.C. and giving it back to you, the people. For too long, a small group in our nation's capital has reaped the rewards of government while the people have born the cost. Washington has flourished, but the people did not share in its wealth. The establishment protected itself, but not the citizens of our country. Their victories have not been your victories. Their triumphs have not been your triumphs. There was little to celebrate for struggling families all across our land. That all changes starting right here and right now. This moment is your moment, it belongs to you. It belongs to everyone gathered here today and everyone watching all across America. This is your country."

Inauguration Address
Washington DC
20th January 2017

"President Obama campaigned hard (and personally) in the very important swing states, and lost. The voters wanted to MAKE AMERICA GREAT AGAIN!"

Twitter
27th December 2016

"So we have to rebuild our infrastructure, our bridges, our roadways, our airports. You come into La Guardia Airport, it's like we're in a third world country. You look at the patches and the 40-year-old floor. They throw down asphalt, and they throw… You look at these airports. We are like a third world country. And I come in from China and I come in from Qatar and I come in from different places, and they have the most incredible airports in the world. You come back to this country and you have LAX, disaster. You have all of these disastrous airports. We have to rebuild our infrastructure."

Presidential Announcement Speech
New York
16th June 2017

"We are going to fix our inner cities and rebuild our highways, bridges, tunnels, airports, schools, hospitals. We're going to rebuild our infrastructure, which will become, by the way, second to none. And we will put millions of our people to work as we rebuild it."

Election Victory Speech
New York
9th November 2016

"The world was gloomy before I won - there was no hope. Now the market is up nearly 10% and Christmas spending is over a trillion dollars!"

Twitter
26th December 2016

"Crumbling infrastructure will be replaced with new roads, bridges, tunnels, airports and railways gleaming across our very, very beautiful land. Our terrible drug epidemic will slow down and ultimately stop. And our neglected inner cities will see a rebirth of hope, safety, and opportunity. Above all else, we will keep our promises to the American people."

Congressional Speech
Washington DC
28th February 2017

"The U.S. Consumer Confidence Index for December surged nearly four points to 113.7, THE HIGHEST LEVEL IN MORE THAN 15 YEARS! Thanks Donald!"

Twitter
27th December 2016

"Jobs are returning, illegal immigration is plummeting, law, order and justice are being restored. We are truly making America great again!"

Twitter
12th April 2017

"One by one we are keeping our promises - on the border, on energy, on jobs, on regulations. Big changes are happening!"

Twitter
12th April 2017

"Everything that is broken in our country can be fixed. Every problem can be solved. And every hurting family can find healing, and hope."

Congressional Speech
Washington DC
28th February 2017

"Economic confidence is soaring as we unleash the power of private sector job creation and stand up for the American Workers. #AmericaFirst"

Twitter
12th April 2017

"We stand at the birth of a new millennium, ready to unlock the mysteries of space, to free the Earth from the miseries of disease, and to harness the energies, industries and technologies of tomorrow. A new national pride will stir ourselves, lift our sights, and heal our divisions."

Inauguration Address
Washington DC
20th January 2017

"When we celebrate our 250 years of glorious freedom, we will look back on tonight as when this new chapter of American greatness began."

Congressional Speech
Washington DC
28th February 2017

"Together, we can save American lives, American jobs, and American futures. Together, we can save America itself. Join me in this mission to Make America Great Again."

Campaign Rally
Phoenix Arizona
31st August 2016

On political correctness:

"Look at evangelicals. You can't even use the word 'Christmas' any more. Macy's don't use the word 'Christmas' any more. I mean, you can't even use the word 'Christmas' any more. And you know, with me, it's going to stop. It is going to stop, and they understand that."

The Economist
3rd September 2015

"It's very time consuming to be politically correct, and I don't have the time. It's also very boring to be politically correct."

The Hollywood Reporter
19th August 2015

On trade unions:

"If United Steelworkers 1999 was any good, they would have kept those jobs in Indiana. Spend more time working-less time talking. Reduce dues"

Twitter
7th December 2016

"Chuck Jones, who is President of United Steelworkers 1999, has done a terrible job representing workers. No wonder companies flee country!"

Twitter
7th December 2016

The Intelligence Community

In which Mr Trump shares his thoughts on the FBI, the CIA and the NSA

"The 'Intelligence' briefing on so-called 'Russian hacking' was delayed until Friday, perhaps more time needed to build a case. Very strange!"

Twitter
3rd January 2017

"Intelligence agencies should never have allowed this fake news to 'leak' into the public. One last shot at me. Are we living in Nazi Germany?"

Twitter
11th January 2017

"The real scandal here is that classified information is illegally given out by 'intelligence' like candy. Very un-American!"

Twitter
15th February 2017

"Thank you to Eli Lake of The Bloomberg View – 'The NSA & FBI...should not interfere in our politics...and is' Very serious situation for USA"

Twitter
15th February 2017

"Information is being illegally given to the failing @nytimes & @washingtonpost by the intelligence community (NSA and FBI?) Just like Russia"

Twitter
15th February 2017

"It now turns out that the phony allegations against me were put together by my political opponents and a failed spy afraid of being sued. Totally made up facts by sleazebag political operatives, both Democrats and Republicans - FAKE NEWS! Russia says nothing exists. Probably released by 'Intelligence' even knowing there is no proof, and never will be. My people will have a full report on hacking within 90 days!"

Twitter
13th January 2017

Donald Trump

In which Mr Trump reveals little known facts regarding his vast wealth, his vast intelligence, his enormous sexual prowess and his hair

"I told you @TIME Magazine would never pick me as person of the year despite being the big favorite. They picked person who is ruining Germany [Angela Merkel]."

Twitter
December 2015

"Thank you to Time Magazine and Financial Times for naming me 'Person of the Year' - a great honor!"

Twitter
15th December 2016

"I'm actually a nice person. I try very hard to be a nice person."

Fox News
28th September 2014

"I've never gambled in my life. To me, a gambler is someone who plays slot machines. I prefer to own slot machines."

Trump: The Art of the Deal
1987

"My life essentially is one big fat phone call."

Esquire Magazine
January 2004

"I photograph short. I'm six-foot-three."

The New York Times
19th September 1999

"I'm only thick-skinned when somebody says bad things that are false."

Fox News
18th October 2015

"I don't like doing a lot of talking. I like...believe it or not...I like action."

Fox Sports
2nd November 2015

"My twitter has become so powerful that I can actually make my enemies tell the truth."

Twitter
17th September 2012

"I've really been focused much more on the news shows lately, on Fox and CNN and even MSNBC, which is doing better because they're covering me all the time."

The Hollywood Reporter
3rd September 2015

"I think I am, actually humble. I think I'm much more humble than you would understand."

CBS News
17th July 2016

On shaking hands:

"I think the handshake is barbaric... Shaking hands, you catch the flu, you catch this, you catch all sorts of things."

Time Magazine
8th November 1999

"The concept of shaking hands is absolutely terrible, and statistically I've been proven right."

Playboy Magazine
October 2004

"Something very important, and indeed society changing, may come out of the Ebola epidemic that will be a very good thing: NO SHAKING HANDS!"

Twitter
4th October 2014

"Know what? After shaking five thousand hands, I think I'll go wash mine."

New Yorker Magazine
19th May 1997

On family:

"My marriage, it seemed, was the only area of my life in which I was willing to accept something less than perfection."

Surviving at the Top
1990

"I was always very much accepted by my father. He adored Donald Trump."

Playboy Magazine
March 1990

"I want five children, like in my own family, because with five, then I will know that one will be guaranteed to turn out like me."

Vanity Fair
September 1990

On his daughter, Ivanka:

"@Ivanka Trump is great, a woman with real character and class."

Twitter
16th January 2017

"At 9:00 P.M. @CNN, of all places, is doing a Special Report on my daughter, Ivanka. Considering it is CNN, can't imagine it will be great!"

Twitter
16th January 2017

"She does have a very nice figure… If she weren't my daughter, perhaps I'd be dating her."

ABC News
2006

"You know who's one of the great beauties of the world according to everybody? And I helped create her. Ivanka. She's six feet tall, she's got the best body. She made a lot of money as a model – a tremendous amount."

The Howard Stern Show
2003

"Every guy in the country wants to go out with my daughter."

New Yorker Magazine
13th December 2004

On golf:

"Let golf be elitist. When I say 'aspire,' that's a positive word. Let people work hard and aspire to someday be able to play golf."

Twitter
1st July 2015

"I don't think I'm going to lose [the election], but if I do, I don't think you're ever going to see me again, folks. I think I'll go to Turnberry and play golf or something."

Campaign Rally
Maryland
24th April 2016

On his vast wealth:

"I say, not in a braggadocios way, I've made billions and billions of dollars dealing with people all around the world."

CNN
16th September 2015

"I was a businessman all my life. I've made a tremendous fortune."

ABC News
2nd August 2015

"Some people have a talent for piano. Some people have a talent for raising a family. Some people have a talent for golf. I just happen to have a talent for making money."

Playboy Magazine
October 2004

"People say the 80s are dead, all the luxury, the extravagance. I say, 'What? Am I supposed to change because it's a new decade?' That's bullshit!"

Playboy Magazine
March 1997

"I look very much forward to showing my financials, because they are huge."
Time Magazine
14th April 2011

"If you don't tell people about your success, they probably won't know about it."
Trump: How to Get Rich
2004

"Part of the beauty of me is that I am very rich."
ABC News
17th March 2011

On his vast intelligence:

"I am a really smart guy."
Time Magazine
14th April 2011

"I'm intelligent. Some people would say I'm very, very, very intelligent."
Fortune Magazine
3rd April 2000

"Sorry losers and haters, but my IQ is one of the highest, and you all know it! Please don't feel so stupid or insecure, it's not your fault."

Twitter
9th May 2013

"I know some of you may think I'm tough and harsh but actually I'm a very compassionate person (with a very high IQ) with strong common sense."

Twitter
21st April 2013

"Who knows what's in the deepest part of my mind?"

BuzzFeed
13th February 2014

"I'm a very smart guy. I went to the best college. I had good marks. I was a very smart guy, good student, all that stuff."

The O'Reilly Factor
2011

"A lot of people see psychiatrists because they don't have enough on their mind. I spend so much time thinking about buildings and deals and clubs and doing what I do that I don't have time to get into trouble mentally."

Playboy Magazine
October 2004

"I never fall for scams. I am the only person who immediately walked out of my 'Ali G' interview."

Twitter
30th September 2012

On his temperament:

"I'm also honoured to have the greatest temperament that anybody has."

3rd November 2016

"So I have to tell you this — I have to say it: I think my single greatest asset of any assets I have is my temperament, and I know how to win. But it's my temperament, it's my single greatest asset."

Campaign Rally
North Carolina
6th September 2016

"By the way, she [Hilary Clinton] says things about me that are horrible. As an example, the single greatest asset I have, according to those that know me, is my temperament. But she came up with this Madison Avenue line — 'Oh, let's talk about his temperament.' It's the single greatest asset I have — is my temperament."

ABC News
6th September 2016

"I think temperament is one of my greatest assets. I've won all my life, I've been winning. I always thought that temperament — I mean I have always felt, and been told, that my single greatest strength is temperament."

The La Crosse Tribune
17th August 2017

"I think I have the best temperament, or certainly one of the best temperaments, of anybody that's ever run for the office of president. Ever. Because I have a winning temperament. I know how to win."

Campaign Rally
Colorado Springs
29th July 2016

"And I will say this, on temperament. You know, I think temperament — and a lot of people have said that that know me that maybe my greatest strength is my temperament. And I have a temperament that wins. I have a winning temperament. … I think probably, maybe one of my greatest assets — if not my greatest asset, Kimberly — is temperament. I know how to win, and I have a winning temperament. And that's what our country needs."

Fox News
26th August 2016

"[Hillary Clinton's] got the temperament of a loser. I have the temperament of a winner, and we have to win again."

Fox Business
9th August 2017

"My temperament is so much tougher, so much better than hers."

San Jose, California
2nd June 2016

On his celebrity status:

"I can't help it that I'm a celebrity. What am I going to do, hide under a stone?"

USA Today
27th February 2004

On his sexual prowess:

"I think Viagra is wonderful if you need it, if you have medical issues, if you've had surgery. I've just never needed it. Frankly, I wouldn't mind if there were an anti-Viagra, something with the opposite effect. I'm not bragging. I'm just looking. I don't need it."

Playboy Magazine
October 2004

"Oftentimes when I was sleeping with one of the top women in the world, I would say to myself, thinking about me as a boy from Queens, 'Can you believe what I am getting?'"

Think Big: Make it Happen in Business and Life
2008

"He [Marco Rubio] referred to my hands, if they're small, something else must be small. I guarantee you there's no problem. I guarantee it."

Presidential Debate
3rd March 2016

"All of the women on *The Apprentice* flirted with me, consciously or unconsciously. That's to be expected."

Trump: How to Get Rich
2004

"If I told the real story of my experiences with women, often seemingly very happily married and important women, this book would be a guaranteed best-seller (which it will be anyway!). I'd love to tell all, using names and places, but I just don't think it's right."

Trump: The Art of the Comeback
1994

"Of course, if necessary, I could be married in twenty-four hours. It would be very easy. Believe me."

The New York Times
19th September 1999

"I've never had any trouble in bed, but if I'd had affairs with half the starlets and female athletes the newspapers linked me with, I'd have no time to breathe."

Trump: Surviving at the Top
1990

On watching television:

"I don't have a lot of time for listening to television."

The New York Times
28th June 2015

"If I'm on a show, I'll turn on the show."

CBS News
27th September 2015

"I love just being home, relaxing, taking it easy, watching television. And maybe, necessarily, if there's pizza, that's good too."

Television Interview
26th July 1989

On his hair:

"I get up, take a shower, and wash my hair. Then I read the newspapers and watch the news on television, and slowly the hair dries. It takes about an hour. I don't use a blow-dryer. Once it's dry, I comb it. Once I have it the way I like it – even though nobody else likes it – I spray it and it's good for the day."

Playboy Magazine
October 2004

"No animals have been harmed in the creation of my hairstyle."

Trump: How to Get Rich
2004

"As everybody knows, but the haters and losers refuse to acknowledge, I do not wear a wig. My hair may not be perfect but it's mine."

Twitter
24th April 2014

On his popularity:

"I could stand in the middle of Fifth Avenue and shoot somebody and I wouldn't lose any voters."

Campaign Rally
Iowa
24th January 2016

"The fact is, I go down the streets of New York and the people that really like me are the taxi drivers and the workers."

Larry King Interview
Republican National Convention
1988

"There are two publics as far as I'm concerned. The real public and then there's the New York society horseshit. The real public has always liked Donald Trump."

Vanity Fair
September 1990

"The rich people hate me and the workers love me. Now, the rich people that know me like me, but the rich people that don't know me, they truly dislike me."

Larry King Live
8th October 1999

"Wealthy people don't like me because I'm competing against them all the time, and they don't like me, and I like to win."

Larry King Interview
Republican National Convention
1988

On ego and ambition:

"Show me someone with no ego and I'll show you a big loser."

Trump: How to Get Rich
2004

"I have an ego, but all people that are successful have an ego. I've never met a successful person that didn't have an ego."

Larry King Live
1990

I like the challenge, and tell the story of the coal miner's son. The coal miner gets black-lung disease, his son gets it, then his son. If I had been the son of a coal miner, I would have left the damn mines."

Playboy Magazine
March 1990

"As a kid, I was making a building with blocks in our playroom. I didn't have enough. So I asked my younger brother, Robert, if I could borrow some of his. He said, 'Okay, but you have to give them back when you're done.' I used all of my blocks, then all of his blocks, and when I was done I had a great building, which I then glued together. Robert never did get those blocks back."

Esquire Magazine
2004

"I truly believe that someone successful is never really happy, because dissatisfaction is what drives him."

Playboy Magazine
March 1990

21965569R00090

Printed in Poland
by Amazon Fulfillment
Poland Sp. z o.o., Wrocław